Mogul Recollected

Mogul Recollected

RICHARD OUTRAM

The Porcupine's Quill, Inc.

CANADIAN CATALOGUING IN PUBLICATION DATA

Outram, Richard, 1930-
  Mogul recollected

Poems.
ISBN 0-88984-174-8

1. Mogul (Elephant) - Poetry.   I. Title.

PS8529.U8M6 1993   C811'.54   C93-095105-0
PR9199.3.087M6 1993

Published by The Porcupine's Quill, Inc., 68 Main Street, Erin,
Ontario NOB 1T0 with financial assistance from The Canada
Council and the Ontario Arts Council. The support of the
Government of Ontario through the Ministry of Culture, Tourism
and Recreation is also gratefully acknowledged.

Trade orders to General Distribution Services,
34 Lesmill Road, Don Mills, Ontario M3B 2T6.

Readied for the press by John Metcalf.
Copy edited by Doris Cowan.

Cover is after a wood engraving by Wesley Bates.

Printed and bound by The Porcupine's Quill. The stock is acid-
free Zephyr Antique laid, the type Ehrhardt.

❖ ❖ ❖

This book is for
BARBARA

❖ ❖ ❖

Who knoweth the spirit of man that goeth
upward, and the spirit of the beast that
goeth downward to the earth?
Ecclesiastes 3:21

... The circus was billed as Dexter's Locomotive Museum and Burgess' Collection of Serpents and Birds. It had performed in Yarmouth, Nova Scotia for four days from September 27 to October 1, 1836 and travelled and performed throughout Nova Scotia boarding the ship at Saint John, New Brunswick. In order to accommodate the large circus on deck, two lifeboats had to be left behind. The *Royal Tar* was making her regular run between Saint John, N.B., Eastport and Portland, Maine.

Twice the ship ran into rising winds, and took shelter, the second time behind Fox Island on Penobscot Bay. While anchored there, orders were given to fill her boiler. These orders were never carried out and as a result, while still at anchor, the boiler became red hot and set fire to two wedges inserted between the boiler and the elephant cage.

Because of the removal of two of their lifeboats, all that remained was a long boat and a jolly boat. As soon as the long boat was ordered launched, a great number of persons jumped into it, cut the ropes to drop it into the water, and rowed away from the blazing steamer. Capt. Reed, seeing what had happened, leapt into the jolly boat to prevent the same thing happening. The revenue cutter, *Veto*, sighted the fire and as she drew near the *Royal Tar*, Capt. Reed rowed across to her. As the *Veto* was without her regular commanding officer, Capt. Reed and some of his crew volunteered to take over the cutter and supervise the transport of the survivors from the *Royal Tar* to the *Veto*. Under his supervision, fifty persons were saved.

The circus elephant, Mogul, had refused to jump into the ocean and was pacing the deck while some of the passengers lowered a makeshift raft into the ocean. Just as they were getting

---

An extract from: *The Circus Ship Fire*, compiled by Helen Goodwin, Curator, Firefighters' Museum of Nova Scotia. Published by the Firefighters' Museum of Nova Scotia, 451 Main Street, Yarmouth, Nova Scotia, B5A 1G9, with the assistance of the Nova Scotia Museum, 1977.

on the raft, there was a blast of hot air and burning embers. This was followed almost immediately by the frenzied elephant trumpeting in terror. As he was accustomed to doing in his performance, he stood on his hind legs and placed his front legs on the taffrail. It collapsed under his weight and sent him hurtling down into the sea, right on top of the makeshift raft and occupants, sinking them forever beneath the water. Mogul perished before reaching shore, and his body was found a few days later washed ashore.

Three horses made it safely to shore, while three others circled the ship until exhausted and drowned. One passenger fastened a money belt with $500 of silver around his waist and jumped into the sea, never to come to the surface having been dragged to his doom by his wealth.

Of the 93 persons on board, 61 were saved. The *Royal Tar* sank, a complete loss to her owners as she was not insured. The menagerie also was practically wiped out. No blame was attached to Capt. Reed, and he was highly regarded for his bravery during the burning of the *Royal Tar*.

❖ ❖

❖ ❖ ❖

Memory is merely a minimal condition.
By means of memory the experience presents itself to
receive the consecration of recollection ... For recollection
is ideality ... it involves effort and responsibility, which
the indifferent act of memory does not involve ... Hence it
is an art to recollect.

Stages on Life's Way, Sören Kierkegaard

Backlit by flames, Mogul, the pachydermatous ('thick-skinned; not subject to rebuff, ridicule or abuse' [*OED*]) star of Dexter's Locomotive Museum, who had 'refused to jump into the ocean and was pacing the deck' blared with frenzied terror and, as he had been trained so painstakingly to do for the delectation of the rubes, placed his fore-umbrella-stands on the ship's taffrail. Which gave way under his weight, plunging him into the makeshift raft and its occupants, 'sinking them forever beneath the water.' Forever is a long time, we must admit. Amen.

In the event, almost all ('Three horses made it safely to shore, while three others circled the ship until exhausted and drowned') of the unfortunate heathen beasts, including Burgess's Collection of Serpents and Birds and the passenger who '...fastened a money belt with $500 of silver around his waist and jumped into the sea never to come to the surface, having been dragged to his doom by his wealth', perished along with Mogul. However, thanks largely to the gallantry of Captain Reed, Master of the *Royal Tar* ('... a complete loss to her owners as she was not insured') sixty-one Christian souls were that day saved. Praise be!

The elephant, it might be noted in passing, is the only animal, other than man, that can weep.

O were this animal world otherwise narrated.
As it may be, God willing, or unwilling
God of our fathers disposing, disposed:

as I, my immense self, Mogul Behemoth, begat
by Behemoth of Behemoth, plunged bellowing
from the burning after-deck of the *Royal Tar*

into the last black waters, my past diminished
to pin-point, my future is flashed forth entire
before my eyes. For here, attendant throughout

untold æons of absence to greet me, my other
Leviathan Bride rising from blackest abysm
and ardent in season receives me! So be it.

And here in the undulant amber kelp-forests,
the heaved ice-water boiling about us, I sire
I Mogul! in sorrow the first kind of our kind

brought forth as foretold: tremendous at birth,
prodigious for increase, displacing the oceans
until the world, lopsided, unbalanced, wobbles

out of its steadfast orbit about the astounded
sun and is flung, spun into ultimate nothing
forever as reckoned by my death. O so be it.

In fact in actual fact I was found drowned
on the shore days later, the bright gulls sated
with elephant eye. That is their whole story.

What in Hell is this, snapped in mid-air? A strange
beast in these maritime parts, friend, I'll be bound:
a bloody great Indian elephant. Old Mogul, no less!

Caught falling head over heels (not in love) above
a raftful of sailors deserting a sinking ship.
It's every man for himself, the jolly boat gone.

And them gaping upwards, transfixed in their horror,
like a damned nest of fledglings about to be fed,
at the trumpeting animal crashing upon them! Consider:

if each of them fathered ten children who fathered
ten children etc.; a whole race of survivors
about to be swamped by the plunged bulk of a beast.

The photographer's phosphor flares from a steel ankle-
shackle, top of the frame; that there's a tusk thrust
centre, under the wild eye, the blown-back-gamp ears;

a snaked trunk near the bottom. Well, takes puzzling out,
a picture like this. Sometimes it helps if you turn it
to down-side up. Then the creature is seen ascending

from flame to an Elephant Heaven past agonized Angels
bending in frozen compassion out of a mess of kindling,
the shucked sins of the saved. It's a judgement, I'd say.

I'd give them Angels gold banderoles, maybe, reading:
'O hear us when we call to Thee ...' and 'Jesus wept'
and 'Breaches the darkness of Ceylon with blares'.

The cod of Penobscot Bay witnessed something prodigious:
an elephant descending. And raised not so much as an eyebrow.

The krill cried out to Behemoth misapprehended: 'Devour!
The red stain of our plenitude will survive even you.'

The sidling crabs gazed askance at this downwards progression;
it was, they concluded, against the one law of their nature.

The cuttlefish were phlegmatic; in the Ur-myth it was written:
their white boneshards would grace the cages of budgerigars.

The wolf-eels, unschooled in titanic shadow, squeezed back
into lightless fissures, tight-knotted together in ardour.

The jealous oysters snapped shut, secreting their nacre lest
this singular mote might, embosom'd, become uncorrupt pearl.

The body of Mogul settled into the silt semblance of death.

In the contemporary wood engraving an elephant is shown;
a floating boulder with a single tusk and an uplifted trunk.
He is menaced astern, it would appear, by a projecting fluke
of the *Royal Tar*'s anchor. The waves are cluttered with junk:

castaways clutching at spars, or going down for the third
and last conceivable time; in the background the ship's boat
pulls a survivor aboard; a gargoyle, the round head of an ape;
three horses thrashing, two black and one white, still afloat.

In Klee's *Angelus Novus* the angel, gazing aghast at the past
is hurled backwards into the future by a tempestuous breath
from Paradise. Here, a passion, an exile, an inconsequential life
in captivity is not recorded. Only the manner of a death.

Rub-a-dub-dub, three men in a tub,
oval, with crooked staves,
bobbing about on an ivory sea,
busy with white-capped waves:

the Father, the Son and the Holy Ghost.
Three horses are swimming around
and around and around and around the tub.
These are the three that drowned;

the three that made it to shore,
and were after a fashion spared,
are crossing the void slicked vortex
where terrified Mogul blared.

And the deeps writhe with serpents
and the surface is churned with birds
of every description, perishing.
And Burgess ballooning the words:

'... and powerful, and sharper
than any twoedged sword';
and Dexter is shown bellowing:
'We are not insured, O Lord!'

And sinking astern, abandoned
by all hands, seen from afar,
with her cargo of creatures captive
below decks, the *Royal Tar*.

Carved over her canted funnels,
ascending from raging flames,
is a blaze-winged angel bearing
an ark's manifest of names.

Down from the Cross, dead centre,
is Captain Reed, with spike-holes
in his gloves and boots: the saviour
of sixty-one mortal souls,

including the born-again boatswain
who incised this in thirty-seven
on one of Mogul's salvaged tusks.
At hand is the kingdom of heaven.

Purple prose from the silver-tongued:
'... dragged to his doom by his wealth.'
I ask you! Who in this world isn't?

At the surface I clutched at a sailor
blowing silver bubbles of terror;
but the cheapskate survived.

One fathom down, I passed a gorilla,
a great silverback male drowning.
In his death he resembled a man.

At three fathoms, I encountered
a white stallion, flailing or prancing.
'Hi-yo Silver!' I hollered at him.

Five fathoms down and I passed fast
a silver-and-amber-greaved adder
tying himself in a last loveknot.

At fifteen fathoms the silver lances
of light from the surface no longer
stabbed at my long-suffering eyes.

Forty fathoms, I met a man with a mere
thirty pieces of silver for his shame.
Friends, I sneered at his poverty.

Wisdom may be golden; but in this world
it's silver that keeps the whole damned
menagerie travelling, believe me.

I like it here at black rock-bottom.
Listen, there isn't enough silver minted
to persuade me to try to rise again.

He was the wife's first cousin, Wallace, out of Moncton.
A sad loss. But what got to her, womanly I'll be bound,
she carried on something fearful at the Memorial Service,
was those caged birds and animals, burned and drowned.

At the General Meeting, Yarmouth, she put in the time
most days at the Locomotive Museum, best part of a week;
took to feeding the elephant roast peanuts, and it seems
the creature reached out its trunk once, stroked her cheek.

It's like any other transaction, can't take it personal.
There's good money to be made in lumber, mining, cod:
but there's no wherewithal in the whole world to ensure
wild beasts against common peril, nor acts of God.

But
when there rained slowly down
beasts and serpents and birds
of every description, from all climes,
and the bodies of men and women,
some burned and disfigured,
the stonecold, older than death
Great Lobster of Penobscot Bay
who hoarded the one Truth
of his massive dominant claw
that could crush basalt boulders
to meaningless gravel,
who fed only on death,
presumed that the frail, bobbing,
all-too-combustible gopher vessel,
that Ship of Fools trinket, God's
Ark, had foundered at last
as he had long prophesied
to those who would listen.

Life in the light,
in the honed winds of the world,
in the dominion of shapelesse flames,
in the tinder above the abysm
being too fickle, too febrile,
too caught up in variation,
too infected with fecund man,
to endure the recurrent
sea-pulse that requires
æons to round and return
to the absolute bone-zero
theme of mortal survival
for ever and ever.

But
what had become, he pondered,
bemused, of the obedient
unfettered elephant sent,
dispatched in frail faith from the frail
bark, sent forth to discover
a landfall, a promised haven?
He must have stampeded,
ascending, blinded by freedom,
into the blazed unforgiving
sun wheeled high overhead
and been instantly cindered:
if not, and had he returned
with the talisman green olive
sprig to the redemption of all
desperate creaturedom, then
he, Lobster Prophet, existed
in a profound, unthinkable,
mortal abysmal error.

I say it shall go out.
Our daystar, from the sky.
This given incandescence must
in time die.

There are no flames upon
which Mogul cannot gaze:
time present past and future
in this blaze.

Time past and time to come
are out of mortal mind.
He who holds the sun's eye
is struck blind.

When I dwelt in darkness
before the seed of light
how was God then remembered
in that night?

If I dwell in brightness
holding burning sway
how shall God be forgotten
in that day?

When I am quenched by death
and the world is one
flame, who will stare down
that last sun?

Now is the one ignition
where Mogul does not die.
I Mogul am immortal ember
in my eye.

Men have survived who have hearkened to our singing
of perfect death. A lifetime, if not for long.
Men are in love with death but they will not know it
until they have been enamoured of our song.

In their beginning was our wordless promise
of wordless rapture; wordless is our refrain
of endless death, endless as boundless oceans
where they may rest as mankind made whole again.

Sweet is our song to sailors above the tempest:
bitter the death of an elephant, lost at sea,
who has overheard, drowning, the mermaids singing
of all that is past, or passing, or not to be.

Mogul, who never forgets, remembers:

grasping his dam's tail with his up-stretched trunk
as they moved warily under the high leaf-canopy
through emerald-dappled light; his butting to suckle.

The endlessly echoing crash of the rifle; and what then followed.

The sweet, slightly fetid stink of oozed sap
from the felled tremendous trees; how the logs
tumbled slowly forever into the sluggish river.

The ceaseless shrill-animal cries of the priests
as the boy God-King, to the groaning of horns
and the tintinnabulations of delicate bells,
mounted the pearl-and-ruby-encrusted howdah.

The fug of the winter tent; the chipped buckets
of tainted water, never enough; the soured straw;
the urinous reek from the wagon-cages of apes.

The squeals of the rats in the black of the hold
as they fought through his leg-chains for scraps;
how the bulwarks battered his flanks in rough seas.

The kindness of daft Percy, the handler who rubbed
a tar-camphor balm of his own concoction on Mogul's
festered chafe-sores night after night, mumbling
Latin tags and snatches of hymns to himself
and sometimes weeping, silently, for no reason.

Burgess kept a golden eagle.
In a wire cage.
It watched God all day.
It did not insofar as daft Percy could tell
put the least portion of Heaven in a rage.
Nor of Hell.

Not that Blake was mistaken.
Not about that.
Nor the vision of God.
Burgess's and Blake's perspectives were twain,
daft Percy would opine. It got fed dead rat.
Now and again.

Plenty of dead rats about
a menagerie.
And God knows how come.
The eagle watched God. Burgess watched the roots.
Elephant Mogul, as far as daft Percy could see,
watched the fruits.

Daft Percy long pinioned saw
no eagle soar.
God sees the eagle fall.
Mogul blaring the raging of the stormy sea can
prove portions of eternity too great for
the eye of man.

No one save daft Percy watched
his Mogul die.
To the present of God.
The destructive sword fallen and his dear Mogul is dead
his dear Mogul and a portion of Genius is soared on high
lift up thy head!

Mogul went on musth and trampled
all of the sacrosanct temples of India
into the mud of becoming.

He sucked up the glittered Ganges,
leaving the great-scaled fishes gasping,
and sprayed semen on the faithful.

He butted the sun into stunned submission,
bolted the white-cabbage moon in one gulp,
and blared for black holes.

He encircled the earth with his trunk
at the equator and squeezed it
into an hour-glass, more or less.

He uprooted Fox Island with one tusk-thrust
and hurled it onto the mainland
where it remains to this day, dripping.

And caught up with the idler from Yarmouth
who fed him three plums and a lit cigarette
when the handlers' backs were turned.

But that is another story.

A competence for daughters; younger sons
went into the professions. To ensure
the family name was not disgraced, and strict
adherence to the primogeniture.

A rare albino male, as rumoured; nor did he
need proffered peg, or reprimand, to bring
himself to squeeze the trigger. Unlike some.
A pukka sahib is game for anything.

Yet Percy, while his junglewallah hacked
the forefoot off, despite himself was sick.
It's in the attic, filled with niblicks, canes,
split cricket bats, a broken shooting stick.

They finished off the heeling bloodied beasts,
out from the mother vessel in small boats.
The Right whale is called right because it's slow
in passage, rich in blubber, and it floats

when dead, so fewer carcasses are lost.
Fin whales are fast and skittish, but you learn
to kill the calf first, and the stricken cow
remains in range, to be harpooned in turn.

Had they, to their amazement, come upon
an elephant, on Mogul floundering, alive
in what they reckon as death's element,
they would have striven as one man to drive

their lances home into his lungs, his heart,
astonished at the thickness of his hide,
accustomed to the quivered quick of whales.
Not that they could have spared him had they tried.

The mortality rate was troublesome: an outbreak of fever
below decks could ruin investors and owners. The stakes
were high: on a fortunate voyage, so were the profits.
The trade required risk-capital, discipline, clear weather.

Consider Dexter's Locomotive Museum, aboard the *Royal Tar*:
an order was not obeyed, the boilers glowed cherry-red,
the shims wedging the elephant cage ignited and flaming
disaster followed. As simple as that. She was not insured.

And who shall be found to shrive us? Mogul is an elephant.
All elephants are mortal. Ergo Mogul poor Mogul is mortal.
The syllogism escapes us. Who shall be found to shrive us?
Not for his death, not for mortal Mogul's death. For his life.

The waters of Holy Ganges
blind the beholder by day
with flashed coinage.
Being unfit to drink.

And provide purification
for the faithful who swarm
by rushlight on stone ghats,
stripped of their dhotis.

No ocean is left undefiled
by his drowning. None.
This is beyond the bounds
of credence to those souls

who stumble on mortal
corruption, the putrescent
carcass of Mogul, washed
on the rocks of Fox Island.

Shall we escape death?
An elephant does not
dwell on such matters:
Mogul was untaught.

Shall we escape life?
One must sink or swim:
Mogul's choice, however,
was made for him.

Shall we escape blame
for poor Mogul lost?
Who then among us
shall count the cost?

On leaving Headlands, Percy was presented
with a copy of *The Book of Common Prayer*;
on onion-skin, in diamond, yapped and zippered.
It travelled with him almost everywhere.

If even with his glasses he can't read it,
he has entire by heart, if left unsaid,
the Litany; the Psalms; the General Confession;
The Order for the Burial of the Dead.

The voices are inhuman, inhalated,
a glossolalia; then the giant cough
sucked up to sudden silence, the imploded
rifle-shot. He turns the sound to '*off*',

and wishes that he had not done those things
he ought not to have done. Of course, in vain.
Half-cut, he runs the grainy film backwards
to see the slaughtered tusker rise again.

The eye of the October storm
was whiteout, blinding snow.
The lashed water was as black
as the abysm below.

In the old spasmodic film
the charging creature shot
crumples slowly to its knees.
What was once is not.

Mogul's death is black-and-white.
Fixed letters on a page
or frozen frames of celluloid.
Blurred with present rage.

Mogul never forgot, Mogul never forgave
the long passage from Asia to America.

In blackness rats no sun rats no moon
no stars rats only blackness rats scrabbling
through fouled straw at his shackled feet.

When he fell asleep, standing, he kept
his trunk curled, against all habit, lest
he be bitten by starved rats. If elephants,
as every schoolgirl, as every mahout knows,
when used in battle as they were by Princes,
sometimes in thousands, had their trunks
injured they became unmanageable, alas,
inflicting more damage on their own ranks
than on their adversaries. They carried
great wooden castles filled with archers,
were used to batter asunder the spiked
gates of besieged towns. Hannibal took
to the Alps for the crossing thirty-seven;
how many survived has not been recorded.
Mogul, by good fortune, was not once bitten
however; or not, at least, on the trunk.

Elephants are, after their own fashion,
cleanly beasts. Cages become squalid
in a sailing vessel's close confines.
Somehow Mogul survived mortal disease:
was heartsick, heartsick and did not die.

Mogul was not unaccustomed to knowing
the world shift as he shifted his weight,
even all weary Asia, but not like this,
constantly, for night after night on end.
But the voyage, unlike the ocean that bore
their vessel in passage, was not endless.

And when Mogul was ushered at last into
the New World, he was blinded by light
for a while and like many an old sailor
stumbled about, having lost for the nonce
his land legs, his elephant balance.
An imbalanced elephant being beyond
comprehension. Blind elephants goaded
are not. This righted itself in time.

Some of the boldest rats scurried ashore,
began to increase apace: they thrived
in God Bless America land of rat-plenty,
where a man has space and freedom enough
to spread himself out like the plague.

It was required once of Pygmy males
that, early in their adolescent years,
they find and stalk and disembowel alive
an elephant, armed only with crude spears

(they were allowed to smear themselves with dung
to mask their human scent). And thus they would
be seen to demonstrate their manliness,
their entry into Pygmy adulthood.

When Percy was returned to English soil
(the British consul kicked him out, despite
his notable connections, as a drunk
who might disgrace the Colony), the sight

of immemorial elms and parish spires,
the ease of his ancestral home, did not
provide him rehabilitation. They
accepted they'd been lumbered with a sot;

and spoke of 'neurasthenia' in the pub
and paid for the repairs. Indeed the gin
and whisky, mealie beer, malaria
and native pox had more than done him in:

but this did not explain why Percy raged
against the County hunt; or, sober, tore
the altar cloth to shreds; or jammed the breech
of Gawain's treasured Purdy double-bore;

or smashed the antique ivory figurine
that Modred had retrieved from Timbuctoo;
or vanished for a fortnight, to turn up,
remanded as a vagrant, at the zoo.

And when he gave the chess set to a tramp,
and turned on Hobbs, the keeper, with a gun,
and threw the billiard balls into the moat,
it was apparent something must be done.

Australia was not on: so, Lower Canada.
All went according to the family's plan
and Nahum Merlin Percival Delisle
became a commonplace remittance man.

He did not write and no one wrote to him.
And when he died while working in Saint John,
New Brunswick, no kin were notified.
His bank drafts, strange to say, were never drawn.

Either is perfectly true: that any elephant may be described
accurately as a wave
trampling the spaced waves of Penobscot Bay, which is just how
Mogul might misbehave;

or as a particle, a single elephant mote in the vast Atlantic
of time as time began
to run out for a shipwrecked elephant in the ambivalent mind
of his observer, man.

It is a nice distinction: one which for some deaths may suffice.
But not for the sight
of Mogul frantic, gasping for blooded breath in his last black
unravelling of light.

Perhaps it should certainly prove somehow not impossible to put
one reflecting elephant opposite another, and for us to stand
midway between them as a disinterested human observer of sorts.
That would be one way to have the dark nub of infinity to hand.

There is, or is there? both infinite regression and progression:
we have in the past constrained elephants in a variety of ways.
Actual elephants, pierced by the arrow of time, may constrain
variety, as best we understand it, only to the end of their days.

A world, or is it the world? began the instant that Mogul was born.
One of an infinite possible number, however things are viewed,
of possible improbable or, possibly, impossible probable worlds.
It ended for us forever with his death. Nothing is that skewed.

As a new boy at Headlands, and Thatcher major's fag,
Percy first discovered the need to justify, to himself,
the pernicious ways of Man to God. It took some doing.

It was not until, during prep with the lower fifth,
he encountered the conundrum: 'How does one put
six elephants into a Morris Minor?' that he felt
that he had grasped something of the niceties
of theodicean argument (he had not as yet read
The Confessions) in the sophistical rejoinder:

'Three in the front, three in the back.'

Percy, in common with most of the lower fifth,
contracted nits, *Pediculus humanus*;
Matron coped admirably, however; many
of the boys' parents went uninformed.
When, decades later, Percy picked them up
in a doss-house in Nairobi, he rejoiced
that they were not, thank heavens, cooties.

When Dexter discovered, not long after
a furtive visit to a brothel in Yarmouth,
that he had a dose of crabs, *Phthirus pubis*,
and was constrained to request of a smirking
apothecary's assistant in Salem a small tin
of blue ointment, he was further convinced
of the utter vileness of all woman's flesh.

Burgess has, but he does not yet know it,
another snake in a snake in a snake:
a many-segmented *Cestoda*, growing apace,
the fruit of a low fondness for chipolatas.

Mogul harboured, as a matter of course,
a colony of elephant lice, *Haematomyzus*.
Which in its wisdom considered itself to be,
despite a high mortality rate, immortal.
Not without reason. However, although
some members survived prolonged immersion
in the freezing waters of Penobscot Bay,
when they came ashore on Fox Island
they found, specialists that they were,
no amenable host to hand and perished,
unremarked and, like Mogul, unlamented.

Over the years Burgess had done his damnedest
to add it, despite the cost, to his Collection;
nothing attracts the curious like the sure
and certain hope of death and resurrection.

In the event it was not a mishap, however,
that even a Phoenix was likely to survive:
most were drowned, beating against their cages,
if some, battened below, were burned alive.

It was certainly worth the modest price of admission,
for those souls raised from innocence to believe
the tales of inerrant Scripture, to gawk at serpents:
the kind of the Creature that tempted the first Eve.

Having ingested a live rabbit, the anaconda
was sluggish; the chilled vipers anything but dire;
but the king cobras, swaying in their erection,
aroused in some loins an inordinate desire.

Burgess's suits were black and his cravats were sombre;
his pink-flushed prick, his tawny lop-sided balls,
unbeknownst to the public were otherwise sequestered,
lovingly snuggled in genuine snakeskin smalls.

Waves, the colubrine waves in successive momentum
from Asia forever sloughed, pass over the ocean floor
where the *Royal Tar* with her coldblood love has foundered,
to perish as waves must, broken on some far shore.

Some people collect coins, or stamps,
or canes; Dexter collected ankuses.
He had started with scourges but,
fearing he might be stigmatized
as one who practised the English
vice, decided to settle for goads.
Among his prized rarities were:
One with a flask concealed in its shaft;
this was his constant companion.
A sword-ankus with a wicked blade
snugged, well-oiled, in the sheath-
shaft. He used it to skewer cats.
A small ankus of polished steel;
plied for years by Gran Harkshaw
in assisting foolish young girls
who had got themselves into trouble.
A tiny ankus, worn on his watch fob,
with which he was singularly adept
at picking locks, which, he observed,
'are designed to frustrate the honest'.
A bespoke ankus of pernambuco,
carved by a violin maker in Prospect,
Nova Scotia; strung with horsehair,
it would serve as a bass viol bow,
'Just in case,' said Dexter, 'I should,
perchance, be inclined to fiddle.'
A clever collapsible ankus designed
to fit into the headbands of sola
topis, for adventurous memsahibs,
stocked by Abercrombie and Fitch.
A massive fossilized ankus used
by Neanderthal or Cro-Magnon Man
(Dexter was rather vague on dates)
to drive mastodons into fire-pits.
At least, that's what the dealer

in Kennebunkport, Maine, declared.
One fashioned from the broken haft
of a harpoon some say dispatched
the last white whale, signed *Ahab*.
A rare ivory ankus carved
with erotic reliefs: of deft couples
and threesomes entwined in often
incongruous postures, excepting
the C of E missionary position.
Dexter had hoped to run through
the whole gamut, but had given over
with the vicissitudes of middle age,
and an unofficial visit from Chief
Clarke of the Ottawa vice squad.
A gold ceremonial ankus employed,
it was claimed, by King Janmejaya
to deflower recalcitrant maidens.
He had one carved from the helm
of the *Marie Celeste*; to his great
annoyance, it went missing one day
and didn't turn up. He suspected
daft Percy, but never could prove it.
Dexter lacked, and he yearned for
above all else, the stained ankus
hewn from the Cross that Christ
bore on the Via Dolorosa,
inlaid with the fourteen Stations
and three scenic views of Calvary
by an old master, in mother-of-pearl.
He heard tales of its whereabouts
for decades, but it never surfaced
in the salesrooms. In any event,
he consoled himself, it was unlikely
that someone of his modest means
could ever afford to possess it.

O rustic bumpkins, haste and join
the swelling throng, for one thin dime!
No Skylark thrills on fired wings
aloft, no sylvan Throstle sings,
no Dove of Araby shall chime,
as sweet as chink of coin!

My steel may mesh the Kestrel in
abeyance from his fell preserve,
the listless Eagle on his spar
whose tawdry pinions droop is far
from azure heaven; but they serve
to make the turnstiles spin.

The doors will open, friends, at eight
and close at midnight by the clock!
But let the Judas Crow cry 'Jug!'
and every shambling village mug
who knows no Heron from a Hawk
will pay up at the gate.

For but a tenth of one buck (plus
an extra nickel), you may gaze
upon the rarest fowl of all,
the flightless Dodo, kept in thrall
beyond extinction here! (It pays
to guise a Bustard thus.)

Each night I close my ledger's page,
and say a meet prayer, ere I sleep,
for Peacock, Hummingbird and Linnet;
I tell you, there's rare profit in it
for any soul who dares to keep
a Redbreast in a cage.

A mottled living zipper
that does not come undone:
though two entwined within the mind
of many who are one.
As animate as is the moon.
As torpid as the sun.

From egg I am delivered
and unto egg I go.
And in between where I am seen
in sideways forwards flow,
man marks my passage as his own,
or terror-swift, or slow.

And all men start before me.
The venom I secrete,
that can unmesh the staggered flesh
of man from skull to feet
is someone's horror, someone's balm.
I am another's heat.

In winter I lie frozen,
cold-knotted with my kind,
black in my den that mortal men
may find me hard to find,
for they would smash me where I sleep,
as close as death, as blind.

In the white pulse of summer
I bask, become the fire
of broken stone and blood and bone
consumed, immortal pyre
reflected in my seldom eye
to which all men aspire.

When asked, after, by Burgess,
who held no strong views one way
or the other on the matter, why
he had done it, at no little risk
to life and limb (Bettina had been
stoutly trussed according to his
instructions, but the only available
stepladder was decidedly rickety,
and Dexter was no spring chicken);
and was he aware that the law
of the land, and to some extent,
public opinion, frowned on such
practices, however widespread
they might be, Dexter replied
that he had done it, Goddamn it,
so that he could say that he had!

Which made perfectly good sense
in human terms. And moreover
Bettina had been completely
indifferent throughout the act:
what was another inspecting trunk
more or less to an elephant cow?

He trains elephants to perform
their conditional animal acts
before all of the Crowned Heads
of Europe and Lake Chautauqua.
This argues a knowledge of how
best to commingle torment
and gratification. He may
well come to discover himself
imbalanced, however, perched
at the narrow vertiginous end
of the world's teeter-totter,
not daring to move a muscle.

He sells rare animal parts
to unscrupulous apothecaries;
illegal, perhaps, but someone
must meet the growing demand
for the mooted rejuvenation
of jaded libidos and livers.
He may yet himself savour
the gall of an elephant.

He breeds against very need.
His progeny infest elephant
habitat, burning the forests,
uprooting the thorny scrub.
And the seasonal rains come
as they must to scour barren
the slashed hillsides. Mouths
must be fed, at whatever the cost;
who would defy that logic?
Not, certainly, an elephant,
beset by a human cancer.

His is a vicious circle:
he sets cunning snares
on the forest floor for
the legs of elephants.
His fine wire is stronger
than the stoutest hawser;
the more the beast struggles,
the deeper the steel tightens,
the deeper the steel bites
into the tender flesh; and
he nears with each capture
the end of his own tether.
And dreams, by day, of finding
the lost elephant graveyard
littered with skulls housing
gargantuan yellowing tusks.
In the meantime he poaches
by night, with tacit approval.
It is an established trade;
with its fleets of suave white
Bentleys that travel the one
crazed road from the palace
to the adjacent airport.
Lakhs of tourist trinkets,
shoe-horns, letter-openers,
fat Buddhas in samadhi,
intricate netsuke, all
the ricocheted billiard balls
of the world will not glut
the black market for ivory.

He leads the clean-shaven,
slightly hung-over gentlemen
(and often their ladies)
in khaki safari suits to where
they may safely shoot elephants.
For fun, on the one hand, and
considerable profit on the other.
The which they do. Only trophy
heads are taken, of course. And
afterwards, relaxed by the camp-
fire, over drinks, he discourses
on quotas and culls and the great
tusker that got away, and the good
old days when the bearers were not
yet unhappy. And he retires early,
and goes to his canvas cot to sleep
alone, the deep untrammelled sleep
of the righteous professional.

He sells elephant calves
to importunate foreign zoos.
Which necessitates the killing
of the rampaging parent.
The mortality rate is high;
the profits are satisfactory.
They are shipped abroad under
quarantine, with correct papers.
Once there they may, or again
may not, given the limited gene
pool, enable one endangered
species to survive the duration.

And life, as every schoolboy oozie knows,
is '... poor, nasty, brutish, and short'.
Too short, by far, to allow a trained bull
the luxury of three months off work.

The solution is simple, practical and cheap:
starvation. So Mogul was stoutly fettered
to a teak bole and provided only with short
rations of water. When in due course his knees
buckled under his bulk, and malnutrition
had done the trick, he came off musth.

And the floor of the teeming rain forest,
the ground before and about him, in a circle
that marked the uttermost reach of his trunk
strained in his chains, was left swept barren,
denuded of even the least green frond.

Having planted a bullet in the shoulder-bone of an elephant, and
caused the agonised creature to lean for support against a tree, I
proceeded to brew some coffee. Having refreshed myself, taking
observations of the elephant's spasms and writhings between the
sips, I resolved to make experiments on vulnerable points, and
approaching very near, I fired several bullets at different parts of
his enormous skull.
    Gordon Cummings,
    quoted in Mark Twain, *More Tramps Abroad*

There is this to be said of torturers: that they may proceed
in a spirit of clinical detachment, having inquiring minds.

That they may display patience and, wise practitioners,
will not be hurried, but have learned to pause in their labours
for refreshment and reflection.

That they do not limit their ministrations to others, but practise
upon their own kind, not excluding their children.

That empowered by old expediencies and new technologies
they flourish, normalized, in the climate of our time.

> *For that which befalleth the sons of men*
> *befalleth beasts; even one thing that befalleth*
> *them: as the one dieth, so dieth the other;*
> *yea, they have all one breath; so that a man*
> *hath no preeminence above a beast: for all* is
> *vanity.*
>   Ecclesiastes 3:19

> Musth has condemned bull elephants – and, to a very large
> extent, elephant breeding – in this country. Dozens of young,
> healthy males have been executed, by gunshot, poison, and even
> hanging ...
>
> Sallie Tisdale, *The Only Harmless Great Thing*

Life, Mogul reflected, is certainly full of pitfalls.
His grandsire, in point of fact, died in one, his lungs
pierced by sharpened stakes. It took a long time:
but native hunters are nothing if not patient.
And most of the millet harvest was trampled flat.
Better, perhaps, than the slower agonized death
by poison; ripe bananas laced with battery acid
were most favoured: fruits of our civilization.

But hanging! Hanging twelve thousand pounds, say,
of thrashing, convulsing bull elephant by the neck!
What a challenge for Jack Ketch, or William Calcraft,
or William Marwood, who invented the long drop!
But man, who has learned to flense the eighty tonnes
of a Blue whale in a few hours, is most ingenious
in these matters; has steam winches and steel-wire
cables and durable cargo booms at his service.

When a man is hanged, in civilized countries, the noose
is placed so that the drop will break, it is hoped,
his neck and death will be, if not immediate, swift.
But an elephant hanged must asphyxiate. Slowly.

When Eloise Berchtold was gored to death by Teak,
who was going on musth, in Maple Leaf Gardens
in Toronto in nineteen seventy-eight, he stood guard
over her body, until he was shot by the Mounties.
What a golden opportunity missed, for the thousands
of spectators present. For as Mogul had asked himself:

why? Why hanging? To save ammunition? Hardly;
bullets are cheap. And not to save time, nor labour;
the carcass must still be disposed of somehow,
a problem of some dimension. The answer, as Mogul
knew in his bones, is simple. Man is vindictive.
And as Mogul remembered, man, in his terrible
boredom, craves spectacle. In the *venationes
bestiarum Africanarum* held by Augustus, thirty-
five hundred creatures were slaughtered. Pompey,
to gain *dignitatis*, once pitted seventeen elephants
against Gaetulians armed with javelins. And this,
it must be noted, sickened even the Roman mob.

Well, times have changed. And we hang elephants.
How would the inventive ancients have managed?
They had ropefalls, of course; or could, at a guess,
have goaded a suitably trussed bull over a precipice.
But the Gardens had the requisite tackle. Imagine
watching Teak being throttled, dangled spinning
on high from the girders, bright in the gloom,
caught by crossed follow-spots, hung by the neck
from the overhead girders until dead, while Ruby
Ramsay Rouse played Kettelby below! Now that
would be something to tell one's grandchildren.

Suddenly Mogul flehmened, grimacing! Bettina!
Come into her oestrus again, right on schedule;
as sure as God (who, it has been argued, disposes
such intimate matters) made little green apples!

Died in a Neanderthal fire-pit in Pedmont, Moravia.
Died when driven into quicksand by enraged millet farmers.
Died in battle, pitted by Porus against Alexander's dreaded
  Macedonian phalanx.
Died from the spears of Masai youth, newly circumcised
  on entering the warrior class, to prove their manhood.
Died in a log deadfall in Burma, her neck broken.
Died in a burst of machine-gun fire from a chartered helicopter.
Died in the stampede in a *keddah* roundup in Sri Lanka.
Died when an over-anxious sportsperson mistook her for a bull
  on a very expensive big game safari.
Died from a pharmacopoeia of native poisons, cunningly introduced
  into her favourite browse.
Died in a salvo of automatic rifles during an official cull.
Died of starvation when the end of her trunk was severed
  in a wire trunk-snare.
Died of septicaemia from suppurating fetter-sores.
Died when hit by an articulated lorry, while crossing the highway
  by night to the last accessible water-hole.
Died of salmonellosis resulting from slovenly husbandry
  in a fly-by-night circus.
Died of rabies from the trunk-bite of an infected village dog.
Died when bombed by British aviators during the invasion
  of German East Africa.
Died when her vulnerable underbelly was riddled with nails, bolts
  and other bits of hardware from the blast of a blunderbuss.
Died of thirst when familiar rivers were diverted for agriculture.
Died of tetanus contracted through wounds from a crossbow bolt
  dipped in battery acid.
Died, not alone, in a Roman arena, killed by Commodus himself.
Died in a flash flood caused by the clearcutting of the rain forest.
Died swathed in flaming canvas in Hartford, Connecticut.

Lived long enough to bear one bull calf, Mogul: he
  died without get, drowned in the icy waters of Penobscot Bay.

It seemed as if the sun forgot to beat,
such sudden silence followed on the shot:
the blares and squeals of rage abruptly ceased
and all of them stood rooted to the spot

until the bole knees buckled and the bull
slumped slowly sideways and the bouldered head
sank to the trampled earth and pivoted and rolled
upon the twitching trunk and it was dead.

The massive carcass, slowly oozing blood,
lay collapsed at last; five tonnes of meat.
To those who'd proved most stalwart in the stalk,
the tongue was given as a special treat.

With ribald comment and salacious zeal
the testes, prized as aphrodisiac,
were excavated and apportioned out,
providing what perhaps they least may lack.

And far into the night by firelight
they gorge on elephant, while it is fresh
and life is good and their bacteria
complete the dispensation of the flesh.

In the tale told by generations of ayahs,
while the punkahwallah tugged with one hand
and scratched luxuriously with the other,

the spoiled, beautiful young English Princess,
in a moment of true compassion, bent to kiss
Mogul as he lay locked in spellbound slumber.

And he turned instantaneously into an elephant,
borborygmous, mud-wallowing, maddened on musth,
with the usual full complement of parasites.

While the Princess, her wicked father the King,
her cruel step-mother, her vain sisters and all
of her white kindred vanished from India forever.

It is rumoured that in the heyday of the Raj
many an indolent ayah administered tincture
of laudanum on the sly to her fretful charges.

Certainly Percy once, in his manhood, awoke
from his dream to find by his camp-cot a huge
footprint, and cried out, ' – Ay! – and what then?'

Mogul sat for a self-portrait.
A pretty conceit, an elephant
limned in miniature, bedecked
with erotic blossom, in profile
upon an oblong ivory tablet.
No expense would be spared: red
gold and lapis and ground seed-
pearl and possibly costly mummy
would be employed as required.
An inspired gift from one Prince
who had everything to another.

But the ivory icon was finished
mirror-perfect: what Monarch,
wielding the blinding power
of life and absolute death
over his subject creatures,
would behold only a terrible
featureless void, a reflection
of crazed fragments of darkness
in otherwise unalloyed light?

And Mogul, having succeeded
beyond expectation, was never
commissioned again, nor forgiven.

The Prince was presented with yet
another concubine, astoundingly
skilled, purportedly virgin.

A dream fulfilled! In blackest space, he sees
the earth that held him massive captive rise
in all its mottled beauty, and huge tears
of rapture well unchecked from his small eyes.

He had not thought to live to find himself,
despite his promised great longevity,
relieved at last of his terrestrial doom:
his constant elephantine gravity.

Near weightless, as in water-holes, he soars
in one bright bound, ecstatic, over crags,
vast fissures, battered craters, and the strewn
spent hardware and the septic garbage bags.

'But in a sieve I'll thither sail
And like a rat without a tail,'
she screeched, 'I'll do, I'll do, and I'll do!'

In this script he was lost at sea.
So he replied, 'Ms. Witch, it's me.
Just elephant Mogul, Madam. From Dexter's zoo.'

'Here I have a pilot's thumb,
Wrecked as homeward he did come.'
Mogul tried to exchange his buskins for his socks.

The Director said, 'Mogul, I know
that you are dumb; but things are slow
at Dexter's Locomotive Museum. And money talks.'

So Mogul found himself at last
before the footlights, in the cast
of warlocks and God only fathoms how he tried.

But on the night, he kept his head
and lost his lines: 'The earth,' he said,
'hath bubbles as the water has,' and he dried.

Mogul was restive, and went fishing in his water bucket.
His trunk being, after all, a sort of prehensile worm.
You never know when a sucker might find it attractive;
so he dunked it in and just let the end of it squirm.

But no one was more surprised than Mogul, he got a nibble,
reared back on his haunches and hoiked out a great whale,
the one that swallowed the Bible's Jonah. Hard to figure
how a creature that big could fit into a galvanized pail.

There are buckets and buckets. Literal buckets; and moral
buckets; and allegorical buckets; and, Mogul had heard tell,
an anagogical bucket containing the whole of ever-abounding
Heaven, with sweet water enough brimmed over to quench Hell.

A whale out of water soon dies, when its cavernous innards
are crushed by its own weight, so Mogul, who had the knack
of survival out of his element, he learned it, summoned
his elephant strength and chucked the expiring brute back.

Daft Percy, who happened along, knowing more than most folk
about the big ones that get away, fished out a little book
from his hip pocket and recited to Mogul: 'Say Wisdom is
a silver fish / And Love' (he had it by heart) 'a golden hook.'

Mogul bellowed on cue and the rubes duly quailed;
the echo returned from the back of the big top
in dubious translation: 'Nunc stans! Nunc stans!'

Mogul sprayed water upon the suspecting clowns
who rebounded every-which-way in canny confusion
and proceeded to plaster him with garish posters.

Mogul lifted Moira, pert in her pink sequins,
onto his shoulders as lightly, as delicately,
as lovingly as if she had been his own lady.

Mogul collapsed on the tanbark in mock death when
Projecto, the Human Cannonball, was fired forth;
he had yet to master the true pratfall, however.

Mogul picked out on the world's biggest xylophone
with a mallet curled in his trunk the opening bars
of 'God Bless America' and the crowd stood proud.

Mogul danced as the brass band played; at almost
the speed of light, but was reckoned ponderous,
preposterous at waltz, as elephant ordained.

The sun was at its zenith,
the day was bright and wide,

the Corps, assembled in its strength,
saluted them with pride:

the Major and his elephant
were going for a ride

into the steaming jungle's heart
where both could not abide.

The elephant, it has been said,
may sport the thicker hide,

but only just; the Major claims
to have God on his side.

And only one of them returned;
the lesser beast had died.

He lifted up a bloody tusk:
'The ways of Man' he cried

'and God and Elephant incensed
will never coincide!'

Mogul, concerned for the Elephants,
and himself, to tell the truth,
scrabbled together his small change,
squeezed into a phone booth.

He talked with the Holy Father
in the Vatican. Who said that
he had in mind an Encyclical
on the question: *Nihil Obstat*.

In Paris, a junior *fonctionnaire*
discoursed at length on 'La loi
économique des bêtes sauvages ...'
and added, 'L'Etat, c'est moi!'

Next, Mogul called the President,
but all he got to hear
was Texas oilman bafflegab,
it being election year.

Then he phoned the Prime Minister
of Canada; who growled, 'There is no
elephant vote worth a pinch of shit
in the whole of Baie Comeau.'

He spoke person-to-Person to God;
but She/He droned on in a blend
of Urdu and Aramaic that Mogul
just couldn't comprehend.

So Mogul figured he might as well
save his money and his breath;
he stuck his trunk in his own ear
and hearkened for kind Death.

Mogul, who in common with most young working bulls
    had been beaten relentlessly for having an erection,
that he might learn not to be distracted from his labours
by the presence of cows in season, considered amplexus.

It certainly works well for some thirty-eight hundred
    species of frogs, most of which, it seemed to Mogul,
    kept him awake throughout the reverberant nights
        in winter quarters in Florida, that 'venereal soil'.
    Well enough also for Dexter, although he did not,
        strictly speaking, want for an intromittent organ.
Burgess contented himself with handing out pamphlets
    on the numerous dire perils of self-abuse, on which
    he could be reckoned as something of an authority.

But the gymnastics of clasping a cow under her oxters
    dispirited Mogul, their combined weights running
to something like ten tonnes. Although, if the ancients
    got it wrong, that elephants breed only in deep water
because of their bulk, the notion was not without merit.
Given the circumscribed nature of circus life, however,
they were not likely to find themselves bathing together.

Mogul was aware that only the fact of an elephant's
    testes being located internally spared captive bulls
from gelding. He was not certain that he was thankful:
    sometimes the whole cumbersome game can seem,
    to a fettered elephant, not worth the bloody candle.

Investigating his water bucket one humid evening
in Florida, Mogul discovered tiny Hyla Panjandrum
ensconced at the bottom. Who held forth:

'I shall fill the world with my glutinous spawn!
Who will not wallow thereafter in slathered fecundity?
You? What are you, spluttering landling? Bah!'

'I am all utterance! Hear! I reverberate orbited planets
with my one syllable: "*Grug!*" This is sufficient,
what-might-have-been bletherer!'

'I dream a purulent slime-bubble as large as my throat.
To contain the omnivorous universe which, when it bursts,
will end. Then you will be nacreous slime-spatter!'

'And should I be turned inside out by death you will find
cold fire; seed-diamonds; the clinkers of suns I have swallowed.
Ponderous carrion, well may you tremble!'

'When I leap, at the last, I shall not be pulled down
from the wheeled constellation Amphibia! Unlike you,
you great ninny, you rooted nonentity!'

'I am that I am in my guts. I am given and taken.
I am past present and future my own boast, belittler.
Who are you, you haverer, so to gainsay me?'

Mogul, whose snite can stun a large dog, considered Hyla
a while, thoughtfully; belched wearily; and withdrew.

The City Fathers get their Annie Oakleys.
Men of the Cloth are not required to pay.
Tuesdays, often slow, out in the boonies,
are always billed as half-price Ladies' Day.

And Dexter, impresario of zero,
schemes by some mismanagement to bring
his elephants, caparisoned in azure,
trunks grasping tails, into a great *Ring*

of pure and endless light and to parade
them centred everywhere because, because,
if nothing comes of nothing yet he dreams
of hearing on his death-bed God's applause.

Oak Mogul, whirled in constant revolution,
carved simulacrum, would extend with each
successive revolution his gilt trunk to snatch
the brazen circle poised beyond his reach.

The Elephant, the most chaste of beasts, may be inflamed
by mandragora; conceived in water, in water he is born.
He dreads the suffocating Dragon and, absurd, the Mouse.
He guards his vulnerable belly against the Unicorn.

And he '... hath joints, but none for courtesy. His legs
are legs for necessity.' Mogul has been taught to kneel.
Not, granted, for courtesy. He sleeps standing, his bulk
shored by an imagined bole. But his necessities are real.

The Pelican rends her breast to revive her nestlings
with her blood. Harried, the Beaver bites off his balls
to escape his pursuers. Puny, but versed in betrayal,
roustabout Percy will lift up Mogul where he falls.

Mogul is not the Royal
albino Queen Maya dreams,
bearing conceived Buddha.
Or so it seems.

Mogul is not Ganesha,
but flesh and blood. His skin,
thick by mortal standards,
is wafer-thin.

The death in Saint John of Percy was in this wise:
Mogul grabbed him and brained him against his cage.
He then proceeded to trample Percy's body.
Mogul was on musth, become elephant rage.

Any experienced mahout would have told them:
you don't go on the road with an elephant bull.
At night; in a compound behind the fairgrounds;
after the last performance. Dexter had pull

with the City Fathers; he managed to hush it up.
Early next morning, daft Percy went on board
The *Royal Tar* swaddled in gunny sacks,
labelled as venison. Well, circuses can't afford

a bad press; had *The Royal Gazette* got wind of it,
Mogul would have been shot or otherwise put down.
And elephants are costly. There was no next of kin.
The best thing was, to get the mess out of town.

So Dexter arranged, he crossed Captain Reed's
palm with silver dollars, for a burial at sea:
slipped over the side by night, no ceremony.
No names no pack drill. Let sleeping Percys be.

And in the event, no one was any the wiser.
Daft Percy was part cremated. Dust to dust.
The wolf-eels got the remainder of his carcass.
And Mogul died, which some would consider just.

Among Percy's effects was a blurred tin-type
of him watering Mogul from a dented pail.
A trick of light or exposure, it gleamed abundant,
might have been anything under the moon. A grail.

Contracts had been signed; future engagements
had been made. And the animals did not troop
two by two, gazing in feral innocent wonder
at human contraption, aboard the *Royal Tar*.
They were summarily loaded, captive creatures
in cages; or led, or if reluctant or timorous,
goaded, singly across the strait and narrow
gangplank onto the chock-a-block oak deck.
The usual problems of boarding the elephant
bull, Mogul, did not arise; for the extreme ebb
and flow of the tides in Saint John allowed
the vessel to sink betimes until Mogul stepped
on a level, dragging his fetters, from solid jetty
to canting deck, across the seam of black water.
Thus Dexter's Locomotive Museum and Burgess's
Collection of Serpents and Birds were safely
stowed above and below decks in almost no time
at all. So great was the animal cargo, however,
that Captain Reed agreed to offload the two life-
boats, which left them the longboat and one clinker-
built jolly to hedge them against marine disaster.

And the sacked forcemeat remains of daft Percy
were quietly stowed below, packed in crushed ice,
lest he come to stink of mortal corruption against
the general weal. Sailors being sometimes the most
superstitious of souls, where death is concerned.

And the townsfolk, who crowded the docks to watch
this departure, did not think to mock Captain Reed,
his First Mate, or their native sons, who were only,
after all, earning their keep, for their arrant folly.
There were storm warnings, true; but the *Royal Tar*
was staunch and, with twin paddlewheels midships
powered by steam, could breast any October gale.

Poncefort, a hack for the *The Royal Gazette*, assigned
to cover the local story, being somewhat the worse
for wear, not one to rise early, missed the event;
but deciding to risk it, succeeded in duping the old
curmudgeon, his editor-in-chief, with a spurious
version obtained, at the cost of a few quarts of ale,
from a bevy of dockland louts. His orotund prose
not only captured the heart of the matter; moved
by the hair of the dog to scale Mount Parnassus,
he wrote:

> Nor did it escape the fancy of
> some of the thoughtful throng of
> onlookers to see, as the tranquil
> procession of dumb beasts pro-
> ceeded aboard the sturdy vessel,
> a new Ark, under the good guid-
> ance of old Noah, in the person
> of stalwart Captain Reed, set-
> ting sail under lowering skies,
> when, of a sudden, Juno's mes-
> senger, sweet Iris, smiled on the
> enterprise, and, to the jubilation
> of all, landsmen and mariners, a
> great lambent arc, that won-
> drous omen of promise and good
> fortune to man from God, a
> many-hued Rainbow, leapt with
> the misted dawn over our bus-
> tling harbour!

Well, the old bugger was always a sucker for a classical
or a Biblical allusion. The rainbow, of course, was pure
invention; a nice fictional touch. It was, in fact, as usual
in Saint John of an October dawn, completely socked in
to the mastheads and pissing down, raining cats and dogs.

Some days he dreams the pinprick sun
gone out and Mogul lost.
Some days he dreams the sun consumed
selfsame in holocaust.

Some nights the pock-marked moon is seen
reflected in his eye.
Some nights the stars retrieve their spears.
But Mogul does not die.

The sun that shudders in the east
from rounding darkened earth
will rise as Mogul wakes again.
There is life after birth.

For Mogul is an elephant
wherein his world began.
His Mogul, if the weary earth
is barren without man.

You are here in the darkness. I scent you.
You scent me. This lunge of desire
should crumple the reeking boxcar
of gibbons that comes between
two who would be immortal.
The monkeys, screeching, fondle
themselves; or copulate swiftly,
when not grooming for lice.

You are restive. I hear you examine,
over and over, your empty bucket.
The ankus wounds in your vulva,
the fetter-sores on your legs,
keep you from sleep. If I tender
my trunk to the end of its reach
to caress and console you, I cannot.

With all of my elephant strength
I would trample this mad ape,
unbalanced man, in his own mire!
But neither will brute rage suffice;
I cannot. O my other, I swear it:
when the last man has been killed
by his own, in an elephant heaven
that was once of this sacred world
you will not, being dead, ever again
be goaded to waltz in a spangled tutu,
or, cringing, be stood on your head.

Some earthly things are elephant-self-evident.
The trampled land, and the heaved oceans are flat,
more or less; there is certainly little need
to consult with Edinburgh to determine that.

There is an eye of fire describing an arc by day
above Mogul. Not even Behemoth Mogul can
stare that eye down. And elephants are terrified
of all devastating fire: even more than of man.

There is a thin, pocked wafer, often misshapen,
but now and again appearing perfectly round,
veering about by night, of a deathly pallor,
that some nights strangely stays underground.

These are the merciless nights of kindled blackness
when vast drifts and configurations ablaze entire
throw down their spears, the bright parallel lances
piercing wandering Mogul with cold fire.

Mogul has an orrery; not, granted, of clockwork.
Deep-sunk in his skull, forever implanted there.
A single sphere, its circumference is boundless
and its centre is every elephant everywhere.

It is a pretty game, and one that delights children:
straight lines are drawn to interconnect the bright
motes broadcast across the black stuff of the heavens,
and behold! what fabulous Beasts wander the night.

Cetus wounded, shuddering starlight lances;
Ursa in chains, a brilliantly baited Bear;
blazed Leo encaged by aligned planets.
But Mogul is not figured. Not anywhere.

Mogul is all brightness. Only a Host of Angels
saw, when he lurched to starboard, the world careen.
Or has watched since for canted Heaven to be righted.
The death of a Creature must be believed to be seen.

How could I have told you or foretold you.
The death by fire and water of your kind
must remain forever unuttered.

Here is the mirror of being wherein
I, blind Angel, dare not peer. And you,
should you choose, you do not choose,

would not see lineament; the universe
abandoned with your first birth
expands beyond the very pulse of light.

Others may see in the abounding
reflection of otherwise other lives
darkened to this or that, but of you,

Creature, should we behold you
suffering your incandescent death
the only vivid image is of thus.

Percy dreamed two dreams, in their succession,
of immolation. And in each of them he died
into the mortal elements of fire and water:
Percy and Mogul abandoned, side by side.

In death by relentless fire flaming Mogul
would succor Percy, and came to kindle him.
In death by whelming water Percy, weeping,
failed Mogul drowning, for he could not swim.

Sleep is a fleeting death. Percy dreamed he wakened
into a desolate dream wherein Mogul was reborn:
a Mogul half-remembered, half-forgotten, goaded
through Gate of Ivory, goaded through Gate of Horn.

When Mogul broke through the solid teak
taffrail of the *Royal Tar* and crashed
down on the makeshift raft and smashed
it to smithereens, sending its makeshift
crew, deserting their sinking ship,
to their doom forever beneath the water,
some of the human survivors claimed
that elephant Mogul, crazed with fear,
fell back on his circus balancing act,
to his final undoing. This was not so.

Unseen by the shipwrecked souls, Mogul,
sagacious beast that he was, had wisely
placed his trust, his bulk, his dear life
in the one bridge in this fallen world
chartered to bear Behemoth's prodigious
burden: the fleeting diaphanous rainbow.

Upon which he passed, perfectly poised,
treading with delicate elephant grace
on the narrow span, on the parlous arc,
out of the vision of flailing swimmers
intent on salvation in this world, into
his sure and certain haven, into his death.

There are stars overhead in the clear night
in given configuration, quivering nail-
holes in the blackness. Some we steer by.

Some have been named after the chartered Gods
and heroes and absent beasts of men's minds:
most are as nameless as furthering black waves.

Men say they are ancient flame, so flared
in the lost past that even God has forgotten
to weep for their first burning. Perhaps.

I see them now. As the heads of the bright
spikes that hold the black present together.
I am on constant watch until they are drawn.

At dawn, when the sun has hammered them home
over dishonoured Asia and Africa, only then
may I go below, relieved for the time being.

That men in their steadfast death may gaze,
blind to the black constellation of Mogul
risen, caged in the light of disgraced day.

Did not survive fire and water, nor earth, nor air;
not the cumbrous elements. Nor did it become
quintessence, numberless as thou seest. No.
It is closed, clothed in darkness for all time.

Mogul's eye was the still centre, the sometime
calm in the loomed elephant rage to be.
Wherein it mirrored the creature sun.

Mogul's eye had looked on eternal light
grooming the endless orient riverine grasslands;
piercing the overlapped canopy of the unfelled forest;
burning stark verticals in high mountain passes;
knifing through chinks in the slats of a boxcar,
holding the motes mingled in shafts of gold;
tangling snarls in the steel mesh of enclosures;
rebounding blaze from a bucket of living water;
quenched forever at last in Penobscot Bay.

Mogul, alone among other beasts,
in common with man, could weep,
and did, real tears from his small eye.
In common with man, not without cause.
He drowned in salt water.

Being not man nor angel but beast, Mogul
saw not through his eye but with it life
in the myriad present: which is immortal.

And he beheld, as he was beholden to,
what he became: his one death.

BARBARA HOWARD

❖ ❖

Richard Outram was born in Canada in 1930. He is a graduate of
the University of Toronto and lives in Toronto, where he is retired
from the Canadian Broadcasting Corporation. He is the author of
Eight Poems (1959), *Exsultate, Jubilate* (1966), *Turns* (1975), *The
Promise of Light* (1979), *Selected Poems* (1984), *Man in Love*
(Porcupine's Quill, 1985) and *Hiram and Jenny* (Porcupine's Quill,
1988).